ELITE
BUSINESS
DEVELOPMENT
SYSTEM

for

LAW FIRMS

*THE FASTEST PATH
TO 8-FIGURE REVENUE*

RONNIE DEAVER

The

ELITE
BUSINESS
DEVELOPMENT
SYSTEM

for

LAW FIRMS

THE FASTEST PATH
TO 8-FIGURE REVENUE

RONNIE DEAVER

Designed by Dino Marino, www.dinomarinodesign.com.

E-book ISBN: 979-8-9893315-0-5
Paperback ISBN: 979-8-9893315-1-2

TABLE OF CONTENTS

DEDICATION

To my incredible wife—not only would this book have been impossible without you, but I'd never have become the man capable of writing it without your daily influence.

You are my guide, my support, and my duty.

Love,
Ronnie

INTRODUCTION

I was on a conference call when I found out. My team and I were meeting to discuss the results of our work with *Guardian & Baron*, an Elder Law firm with a series of offices in the Pittsburgh area. (Note: all names throughout this book have been changed to ensure client privacy.)

It was my first time testing our new Marketing Mastery System product.

I can't tell you how nervous I was to get on that call.

I'd made a big bet that I could judge when a law firm was prepared for explosive growth, and that I could drive that growth.

Sure, that's a big bet for *Guardian & Baron,* you might say, but not for *me*. But no, I mean, it was a big bet for *me*, and my whole team knew it.

I was guaranteeing that we'd be profitable in three months or less. Which meant I had $15,000 on the line. And I was a brand-new company. I would have to cover that personally, or it'd bankrupt the company.

Also, I knew what this meant for *Guardian & Baron*. One of the founding attorneys was deeply burned out on marketing, and he'd come to expect lukewarm results that never merited the effort. I knew he was only giving me a shot because I'd been a guest speaker on a podcast he listened to, and the host had vouched for me. If I didn't work out, his hope for explosive business growth would dive even deeper. I knew what that could do to an attorney and a firm.

My bet was this: I knew why some firms grew explosively and, even more boldly, that I could replicate it in firms that didn't. I picked *Guardian & Baron* because it fit my model perfectly for a firm that would grow explosively if it installed my Marketing Mastery product and would grow extremely slowly if it did not.

Let me run you through what I was seeing. By the end of this book, you'll know why every bit of it excited me.

Guardian & Baron had a strong intake and sales setup already in place. They were closing up to 80 percent of their potential clients before I even met them. However, they could never get enough leads to fulfill the capacity they were ready to handle.

They received less than seventy new client calls per month. They had three office locations, but two of them didn't generate enough calls to offset the expense. They struggled to generate even three five-star reviews in that month.

My employees had spent the day preparing the data into a full report. I joined the call, ready to find out whether my theories would prove true.

And I was astounded. I'd expected success, in the sense that I'd spent years analyzing successful campaigns to figure out what made the best go explosive, but in my heart, part of me hadn't *really* believed such a thing could be known, much less replicable.

Up from three, *Guardian & Baron* were getting *thirty* reviews a month. Sometimes more. In less than six months, they'd begun generating over 300 calls per month. Better, those calls were turning into signed cases. Soon, they were regularly informing us of the cases they'd signed, many of them worth $24,000 or more. That's the price of each *individual* case. They have four locations now.

That's explosive growth.

And that was the proof I needed. I'd figured it out, and I could do it again. And, you can do it, too.

THIS IS YOUR LIFE

Let's get real for a moment. This isn't just about income, business development, or status. At the end of the day, we're talking about your quality of life. Your mental and emotional health. Your family.

Remember why you started down this career path in the first place? In order to have a good life. But what we see in many cases is that instead of giving life, practicing law is taking it away at an alarming rate.

Many lawyers feel stuck in the hamster wheel of too many hours, too much stress, and not enough to show for it. And they often feel it's impossible to extricate themselves from the situation.

A law firm is more than a building, a group of associates, or a client list. It's whether or not you get to retire when you wish, you go out to eat at the nicest restaurants in town, your kids have private schooling, or you charter a private jet.

It's not just a matter of business.

CAN YOU IMAGINE?

What if things could be different? What would your life and business be like if you:

... had more leads than you could possibly serve, making it easy to say no to the wrong clients and work exclusively with the people who are happy to pay you what you're worth?

... had trust that your intake team was closing the maximum number of high-quality leads for you to meet with in consultations?

... had control within the consultation meeting, so you wasted zero time giving out free advice and were able to predict how many clients you would sign every month?

... had confidence in and control over your business growth, confident that you're on track to hit eight-figure status in a matter of years?

It's in your hands. All that and more is possible by installing The Elite Business Development System, which I'll break down in the following few chapters. You'll learn to supercharge the three core components of your law firm's business development to drive explosive growth.

I'm honored to have you along for the ride. And if you read to the end, I'll share how you can save $10,000 on having my team install The Elite Business Development System package into your law firm in as little as one hour.

CHAPTER ONE

THE THREE CORE COMPONENTS

It all started for me in 2020 while I was working with a marketing agency as an SEO Manager. At that point, we were working on over three hundred legal campaigns, doing just about every type of marketing, including Google Business Profile, Google Ads, Facebook Ads, social media, radio, and everything in between.

I was excited by the clients who were generating hundreds of leads per month, but I started to notice a concerning trend.

Sometimes, it didn't matter how many leads we generated for somebody; they would cancel anyway, citing they'd gotten nearly no uptick in new clients.

I could give them a hundred phone calls, but they might only book ten consultations, and be lucky to close two or three clients—a dismal result.

The most obvious suspect, of course, was lead quality. But when I looked into it, that theory didn't pan out. These leads were *qualified*. They were people relevant to the attorney's practice area, looking for help. Which, in retrospect, made sense, because I was generating those leads in the same ways that I'd generated leads for my explosively successful law firms.

I'd have some lawyers who would take the hundred leads I'd given them and turn them into a million dollars. Then, there were others who would take those same hundred leads and could barely make $200,000 per year. The gap was massive and perplexing. It couldn't be the lead quality, and it wasn't the practice area, lead source, or geographic location. Some of my clients worked in the same cities, in the same practice areas, and got their leads in the same ways.

And yet…

I HAD TO FIGURE THIS OUT

I didn't *need* to keep the failing clients. I was an SEO manager. It wasn't my job. The lost clients weren't even from my department. But the mystery of it nagged at me.

Some of my clients were just doing so *much better* than the others.

I was happy for the success of the rare ones who could make it work, but all the others were breaking my heart. I watched what it was doing to my clients to put their hopes and dreams into our marketing schemes and slap them up against a glass ceiling, only to watch their competitors outrun them. We held people's finances in our hands, and I could feel the fact that we weren't 100 percent sure whether our marketing would work for them.

I took a deep dive into the problem. I studied hundreds of law firms. The first thing I did was set up lead tracking. I wanted to track everything: every call, every form that was filled out, every live chat, every email.

If it came from a billboard, radio, website, Google, social media, or even a business card, I tracked it. I knew where every individual lead and client came in from for every individual law firm I worked with.

The data started to come in, and it started to form a pattern. That was when I finally realized what was happening.

THREE CORE COMPONENTS, NOT ONE

I noticed that our best-performing clients looked very similar when it came to the leads they got from our marketing campaigns, and very different when I watched what they *did* with those leads.

My successful clients were a joy to watch. They had great intake systems. They hired professionals to answer the phone, worked with outsourced answering services, or were individually talented and diligent. Regardless of their approach, it was well-systematized.

That gave me a massive clue as to what was going on, especially when I compared it to my lowest-performing clients. On average, 22 percent of calls were being missed. That meant no one picked up the phone at all. Very few of those attorneys ever called my leads back or followed up on a voicemail.

There it was! I thought I'd solved it. All I needed to do was improve our clients' intake process. In the meantime, I started putting together my data on clients who *did* have good intake, because surely, they would be highly successful clients I could use as examples.

Except they weren't. And while improved intake increased my clients' results, it didn't do more than give them slow growth where they'd once been stagnant. I wasn't looking for *slow growth*. I was looking for *explosive success*.

Something else was wrong. So, I made an agreement with some of my clients to allow me to listen in on their consultation calls. I listened to my massively successful clients and my dreadfully unsuccessful clients.

A new problem revealed itself very rapidly.

When my unsuccessful clients were in a consultation, they usually stalled out. They'd spend an inordinate amount of time in their consultation calls for very little or no money at all and rarely signed a case. I was looking at attorneys who'd only get one case for every *ten* consultations they'd given.

On the other hand, my successful attorneys were converting 60 to 80 percent of their consultations into paying cases, often without even spending that much time on the phone.

Eureka!

Suddenly, all my data made sense. I knew right then I didn't have a marketing problem. I had an intake and sales problem. That realization changed my career, and I know it can change yours.

If you're frustrated with your revenue growth, that's the one thing you need to understand:

There are three core components to successful business growth, not one.

Marketing. Intake. Sales.

> *Marketing* brings in leads,
> *Intake* converts leads into booked
> consultations, and then *Sales* converts
> consultations into paying clients.

Altogether, that's business development.

The truth is business is a heavy, heavy lift. One core component alone can't do it. Marketing alone can't do it. That just increases how many times a phone rings out to a full voicemail machine. Intake alone can't do it—that's how often a phone is picked up—it's not money. And sales alone can't do it. Without marketing and intake, who is there to sell to? Law firms with only one strong core component putter along with the same team size and a stagnant number of clients, or stall out completely.

If you're stagnant, look into your *marketing*, *intake*, and *sales* and expect to fix two of them. Possibly all three, but usually, those firms die before they get the chance to find this book. You probably have one core component going for you. But I promise you don't have two.

Two successful core components make for slow growth. With great marketing and intake, even a bad sales process converts enough clients for a business to grow, purely through the high number of attempts. The same is true for law firms with great marketing and sales but bad intake. With enough calls and a high enough conversion rate, your business can survive missing most of its opportunities. With great intake and sales, a law firm will usually generate enough referrals to get by. These firms accounted for all my middling results, and while I usually didn't lose these clients, I didn't make anyone extraordinarily happy either.

Three core components, though? Firms with all three core components in place change people's lives. They grow astronomically. They add millions in revenue, and double or triple their business each year.

That's when what I'd discovered really hit me.

Business could be *understood*. Explosive growth could be understood. Even better, *I understood it*. Now you can see why *Guardian & Baron* was so exciting to me when I took them on as a client. They had their intake and their sales figured out, which meant good marketing would send them sky-high. And it did.

WHY I STARTED MY COMPANY

At that point, I knew I had to create a single product that would optimize all three core components: *marketing*, *intake*, and *sales*. Not only that, but it also had to be a system lawyers could buy that would work for them, right out of the box. No training necessary. My clients had become lawyers because they wanted to *practice law*, not master business marketing or intake or sales.

Which meant I needed to figure out how to turn the best of marketing, intake, and sales strategy into a *product*.

That's why I started NoBull Marketing. I was determined to invent a way to optimize the three core components of business development for law firms without requiring my clients' time.

To get started, I offered a guarantee. If my clients didn't get the results I promised, I would refund their money, *including their ad spend*.

I did that so I could experiment with my ideas and invite people to work with me in a way that reduced their risk. I also did it to keep myself honest. I didn't want to sell a single product or idea that didn't give my clients outsized results. I put my money on the line, betting that I'd be able to figure out how to ensure that my clients made money every time, or it'd bankrupt the company.

The marketing foundation had already been set by my previous experience, so I focused on my intake and sales systems. I kept iterating, working with dozens of different lawyers as I developed the most effective systems.

I just needed all three core business growth components—*marketing, intake,* and *sales*—to work in tandem. I knew if I could figure it out for one client, I could do it for others.

I experimented with intake training, which went horribly. And I settled on a new method to combine outsourced labor with dedicated receptionists. I'll discuss those methods in detail in just a moment.

Sales worked very similarly. At first, I worked with my clients, experimenting with them on how I could get them to do better at sales, whether working with them directly or hiring someone for them.

Eventually, I discovered that I could reduce the process down to proprietary scripts that included sales methodology baked into the process. That way, my clients didn't have to already be excellent salespeople to get excellent results. If they followed the script, they would close at a much higher rate than they ever had before. I'll discuss the framework for those scripts in Chapter Two.

And, of course, throughout all of this, I implemented high-quality automation and follow-up. This ensured that anyone using the system aggressively followed up with people from the initial contact point all the way through the sale without them having to touch a button. The emails, texts, and calls would send themselves.

I bundled everything I did into a single product our clients could download into their business with less than an hour of effort, and thus, The Elite Business Development System for Law Firms was born.

YOU CAN DO THIS, TOO

It was incredible. The Elite Business Development System successfully replicated the world-class results I was seeing with my highest-performing clients.

Those clients didn't really know what made them special, but now I did. Even better, I had a replicable system that could be installed into a law firm without anyone having to reinvent the wheel.

Now it's your turn to be excited because from here forward in this book, I'll teach you how to immediately install The Elite Business Development System into your law firm. That means that in your hands right now, you have everything you need to know to scale your business up to eight figures and beyond.

Give The Elite Business Development System three months, and it will pay for itself. Give it a year, and it will change your life.

Let's get started.

CHAPTER TWO

THE ELITE BUSINESS DEVELOPMENT SYSTEM FOR LAW FIRMS

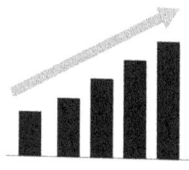

The trick to optimizing a *three-component* system is obvious: optimize each component.

Incidentally, it's also where I also began when I started my company.

More specifically, I began by trying to optimize my clients' first core component: their marketing. Partly because marketing was my bread and butter, but mainly because I had a single piece of knowledge that'd dragged at me for years: most marketers were wasting boat-tons of their client's marketing budgets. Sometimes, even the *majority* of their clients' marketing budgets.

Let's back up a few years before I started my company when I was hired on as a SEO manager at that marketing agency I mentioned before. Now, before I go any further, I want to make it clear that there was nothing wrong with this agency, and honestly, I think we did fairly good work.

But...

Do you remember how I mentioned that we handled our clients' Google Business Profiles, Google Ads, billboards, radio ads, social media pages, and everything in between?

That sounds great to a lot of lawyers—it's all-inclusive! The shotgun approach! *Buuut*, you've got to fire a lot of metal out of a shotgun to hit anything at all.

I had a feeling that a lot of the ads, billboards, and social media pages we made were wasted effort—and money. And so, in my first couple of weeks at the company, I reinvented how we tracked leads and made sure the system got applied to all 300 of the company's clients. I didn't want a single lead to come into one of those 300 firms without me knowing 100 percent where it came from, whether that was a phone call, a business card, a form fill, or a live chat message.

I thought I was going to find out that one or two approaches were underperforming, like, say, billboards weren't worth it, or the radio ads were old-fashioned.

I was blown away by the reality of the problem. Eighty-seven percent of the results we were getting for our clients—*87 percent* came from just 20 percent of our approaches. Every other approach we attempted, from writing blogs to running LinkedIn Ads, *added together*, were only generating that last 13 percent.

But I didn't have the power to fix it. It wasn't my right to kill off giant sections of this agency, even if I did want to go around slashing departments and redirecting employees to the methods that worked.

This meant that despite all the information I had, we never doubled down on the methods that worked for our clients.

If God was trying to motivate me to start my own business, He couldn't have picked a better motivator. I was *right*—I knew what worked—and I needed to *fix this*.

Fast forward two and a half years to when I was starting my company and put my money on the line, betting that I could optimize my clients' three core business development components. Obviously, I started with marketing, and the three marketing assets that I knew drove 87 percent of the results.

If you want to optimize your marketing, I recommend you do the same. Focus on the three most efficient digital assets in the game. That's these three:

Google Business Profile,
Google Ads, and Webinars.

(Note: Google Business Profile was branded "Google My Business" until November 4th, 2021.)

CORE COMPONENT NUMBER ONE: MARKETING MASTERY SYSTEM

Are you surprised by which assets drive over 80 percent of the results? Google Business Profile, Google Ads, and Webinars? Most people don't think Google Business Profile would be in the top three. And most attorneys think Facebook *must* be in the group. Who *hasn't* heard of its power?

But Google Business Profile, the little map thing at the top of a Google search? Some of my clients didn't even know what it was called, much less how to optimize it.

I knew from the start Google Ads were going to be a hard sell. My clients had almost all had a bad experience with Google Ads. They were all poking me to work with Facebook.

But *webinars?* That's where I really went off the deep end for people.

However, it was my company—my money on the line—my product. For once, I got to experiment with what *worked*. And make a product that worked.

So, I set off to forge those three highest-performing marketing platforms into a single product that would send my clients' companies skyrocketing. I dove into the three assets I'd chosen, learning everything I could about why they were underrated, why they performed so well, and most importantly, how to get them to perform even better.

So, let's talk about how to get these three money-makers working for you.

GOOGLE BUSINESS PROFILE

I'll start with what you probably *don't* know about Google Business Profile (GBP).

It's like the front door to your business. It's the first thing your customers see.

If you hand someone your business card and they're interested, they're going to Google your firm, and will end up seeing your GBP listing. If I run an ad for you, they're likely to Google your business name and end up seeing your GBP listing. Marketers often talk about business websites like they're the first thing clients see, but they're really not. That little map listing (and the review average posted in it) is your front door.

> If you've got three reviews and one of them is negative,
> that's like a bunch of cobwebs on your door hinges and a broken handle.

Yeah, maybe I was able to drive traffic to your front step, but that won't do much if they refuse to walk in.

That's a majorly powerful reason to optimize its functioning on its own. A good GBP listing with a strong and positive review count helps every other marketing asset you put in place because they all funnel leads toward your Google Business Profile one way or another.

But honestly, that doesn't account for its full importance. GBP is a sleeping giant that creates up to 72 percent of law firm leads. *Seventy-two percent*—that's crazy. It *sounded* wild to me at first glance. But it actually makes a ton of sense to me now.

Think about it this way:

Try to recall the last time you wanted to find a restaurant near you.

You almost certainly Googled for it, and then looked at the map and the little list of options on the side, complete with their review count, and picked one. Once you clicked on a result, its profile popped up, including its photo, address, and phone number. You may have even reserved your table *without ever going to its website*.

Once I saw that, I stopped questioning why 72 percent of law firm leads come from GBPs.

Because clients search for attorneys like they search for restaurants. They type "immigration lawyer near me" or "the best criminal lawyer near me" into Google and go from there.

If you want to optimize your marketing, optimize your GBP. Then, look at your Google Ads.

GOOGLE ADS

I've always gone through my clients' campaigns, looking for ways to make them more efficient, as every good marketer does. That used to be fairly innocuous. However, in 2021, I started noticing a frustrating change in the way Google Ads operates.

I kept finding my clients' ad campaigns were paying for search terms I strongly wanted to avoid, such as "how to avoid paying for an estate planning lawyer." This was becoming increasingly common, and I watched as Google kept adding policies and systems to make it harder and harder to prevent it. Where I'd once been able to demand a word-for-word search and exclude all others, I now couldn't. I was suddenly required to accept paying for synonyms, and of course, Google decided what words were synonyms whether I approved of them or not.

It's heinous, and, make no mistake, it's intentional. Google is trying to make money on searches no one would ever intentionally pay for.

I cannot tell you the number of hours we spend fighting back against Google's ad programs. The best way I've found to combat it is to make a list of the keywords we refuse to pay for, comprehensive enough to remove most of the trash searches Google attempts to slide into our campaigns. That list is over 3000 keywords long now, developed over years of running law firm campaigns, and it is a constant source of work for us to keep it up-to-date with Google's latest schemes.

In doing so, we've gotten Google Ads to work for us. For my law firms, Google Ads is easily responsible for 8 to 12 percent of their lead flow. Some of my law firms convert cases from Google Ads for as low as $300 per case.

Most of the lawyers I've met believe Google Ads is a waste of money. I can tell you here and now that it's not. It *can* be extremely profitable. Get it right, and it'll feel like printing money—money in, more money out—on repeat.

That said, it's a great area to look for major inefficiencies in your marketing. I used to recommend that my low-budget clients run their own Google Ads to save money on their campaigns. Now, that is 100 percent nonviable. You'll spend *far* more money on useless ads than you would have on a Google Ads expert, and you'll never come close to that $300 per signed case conversion rate I've gotten from Google Ads campaigns. So, if you're running your own campaigns, I recommend you hire an expert. If you've hired an expert, I recommend you make sure they've adjusted to the new reality of Google Ads and its search practices.

There are two things I'd look for when hiring someone to run a Google ad for your law firm:

The *first* is that somewhere in their sales pitch, they say something along the lines of "Google Ads is now designed to *spend* your money, not make you money." If they cannot discuss *in detail* their approach to fighting the platform to ensure it only targets the highest quality leads—the ones most likely to turn into high-paying clients— then they will quickly give you the Google Ads experience most amateurs have. That's a money drain that regurgitates only the worst, lowest-paying leads imaginable.

The *second* is that their marketing agency is specialized in law firms. It took us years to develop our list of keywords to exclude in each particular area of law, where to enforce price caps, and what terms most justify their pricing. We had to do a deep dive into our clients' businesses to know things like what zip codes correspond to the highest-paying estate planning clients in their city. A generic marketing agency will not have that kind of developed knowledge, and therefore, you'll be paying for a lot of leads that won't pay for themselves.

WEBINARS

Webinars brought our marketing product to the next level.

To tell the truth, webinars weren't something *I* discovered at all. My boss discovered them at the old marketing agency I worked at without even noticing he'd done it.

The marketing agency had been growing steadily based on the standard marketing fare: Google Ads, cold emails, cold calling, etc. Nothing particularly scalable, and nothing that brought its revenue growth into the stratosphere.

And then COVID hit. In the beginning of 2020, it looked like a marketing agency would *have* to lay off employees and would *never* be able to even hold steady in the face of a pandemic. Marketing agencies tend to do very badly during recessions or large market shifts. Marketing is almost always on the docket of the first things to cut out of a budget, and law firms are especially quick to react. Almost immediately, the reports started rolling in of law firm marketing agencies filing for bankruptcy, never to return.

But the law firm marketing agency I worked at? It *boomed*. Explosive, *astronomic* growth, of exactly the kind I struggled to understand in my clients' results.

My boss had done something *brilliant*. A choice that makes me smile to this day.

He started a webinar presenting up-to-date COVID information for law firms. It ranged from the latest news about how COVID was affecting law firms to how law firms should apply to the government paycheck protection program. Over time, it changed to become more marketing-focused, as he got more information about what could help a law firm thrive during the turmoil.

The results were phenomenal. Thousands of lawyers attended every week. The business's email list expanded massively. Where we'd be lucky to get more than two consultations a week before, we were suddenly booking one every day. The business grew explosively.

And then, we continued on with our clients offering the same old marketing methods we'd offered before. I was itching inside.

I *needed* to learn more about what I'd just seen. I needed to learn how to replicate it for my clients. Could webinar marketing be applied to law firms? I'd never seen it before.

Finally, after I'd worked my way up to director of operations, I left that agency and didn't look for another position. I had a *rocket* beneath my feet, and I needed to set it alight and see where I landed.

I knew something I saw very few people even peripherally aware of. If I could get webinars to work for law firms, they'd be the most underrated marketing platform for law firms in the world.

And you know what? I got them to work.

Now, our elite law firms generate an average of 10 percent of their leads from this source alone.

The real challenge was to figure out how to make webinars for my clients *without* them having to put time into it themselves. Remember, I needed my Marketing Mastery product to produce phenomenal results *without* my clients having to put in a ton of effort or learn a bunch of new skills.

I figured it out, and I can tell you with total confidence, that you *can* outsource the work for your webinar. That said, you don't need to. If you're up for it, there are a hundred thousand resources online on how to make a successful webinar, from mic setups to scriptwriting.

I can also tell you with total confidence that webinars are the secret to fully optimizing your marketing. They are *the* selling point of my Marketing Mastery System product.

Webinars are what took the good marketing results I was getting for my clients and sent them rocketing exponentially upward.

Here's the trick:

Not only are webinars profitable on their own, but by asking webinar attendees to leave a review in GBP afterward, our clients are generating thirty-plus reviews per month on autopilot.

That might not sound important to you, but when I go to optimize a client's GBP, the *first thing* I work on is their review count. More reviews lead to explosive growth in leads coming from GBP. It's the main and most important way to optimize it.

Thus, my Marketing Mastery System was born, and it allows my clients to absolutely *dominate* their competition.

Remember *Guardian & Baron*? *This* was the marketing invention I was testing for the first time: my Marketing Mastery System product, complete with made-for-them webinars. *That's* how *Guardian & Baron* were suddenly getting thirty reviews a month. They were from the webinar attendees. And that's also how they'd begun generating over 300 calls per month in less than six months.

That conference call giving me the *Guardian & Baron* growth charts proved that my Marketing Mastery System was working as a *product*, something that could be installed into a business that would instantly optimize its marketing component.

Guardian & Baron, of course, were thrilled by their results. And I was definitely excited for them. But I was also excited because I knew something they didn't. I'd chosen their company as a testing ground because they already had two working core components: high-performing intake and sales systems.

What was I going to build for my clients that didn't have good intake? I was ready for the next challenge.

CORE COMPONENT NUMBER TWO: THE PERFECT INTAKE SYSTEM

I approached intake completely wrong when I started NoBull Marketing. Honestly, I was frustrated. I sent so many leads to my clients' companies, and when they failed, they tended to blame me and the quality of the leads I was sending them, and ironically, I tended to turn around and blame them.

Neither was the right approach. Most of my clients became lawyers because they wanted to *practice law*. I needed to learn how to make it easier for them to do their jobs, not teach them how to do mine. The best part of launching The Elite Business Development System (the "EBDS") product was that I got to fully adopt the problem of business development for law firms because solving business problems *is* the job I always wanted to have.

I knew intake was one of the three core components that would give my clients explosive growth, and it finally occurred to me that I could make it my job to solve it without asking my clients to do anything themselves.

I dove into the issue, keeping in mind that I needed to figure out how to make a product that helped lawyers who, quite justifiably, *didn't want to solve their intake problems themselves* to get the results of the law firms that for some reason had found it interesting enough or approachable enough to master.

I found that most of my stagnant and struggling law firms had no idea how their calls were handled. Nor did they have any numbers for how often they converted leads into consultations. Those with receptionists generally didn't request that information and, if they did, certainly didn't have it top of mind.

By contrast, my highest-performing law firms had their intake systems perfectly mapped out, scripted, and tracked by data. This allowed them to always know and improve how many leads were converting into consultations every week.

How could I possibly get my clients the results of the highest-performing law firms without asking them to sacrifice their vocation as lawyers?

I started as I always did: by tracking my clients' data. I gathered information on every call my clients received. I documented where the calls came from, how long they lasted, and whether or not the caller left a message.

One statistic emerged that changed my way of viewing the problem forever.

> My clients' internal receptionists missed *an average of 22 percent* of the calls they received.

Why? I was flabbergasted. One in *five* of my clients' calls was going unanswered even with a dedicated receptionist working the front desk. My clients were just as shocked by the number. They had no idea either.

I could feel their anger at their receptionists. This was costing them tens of thousands of dollars. But it couldn't be the receptionists' fault. Not if all of them were having the same failure rate across the board.

The truth is, receptionists are *human beings.* When they are on the phone with one lead, they cannot simultaneously be on the phone with another. Sometimes, they need to go to the bathroom. If they're sent on an errand, they cannot also be at the front desk answering calls.

In addition, they are not available 24/7; they have off-hours.

But if you're still missing 22 percent of your lead volume, it is still costing you tens of thousands of dollars.

STEP ONE: OPTIMIZE PICKING UP THE PHONE

I could come up with two potential solutions for my clients. The same two possible solutions you might consider if you're still working with internal office receptionists.

THE TWO SOLUTIONS:

1. Hire more receptionists

2. Hire an outsourced call answering service

Hiring more receptionists isn't particularly practical for most law firms. Unless your lead flow is *insane*, there isn't that much work for them to do to justify their salary. A new full-time employee is an extremely expensive way to cover the gaps in a receptionist's bathroom breaks and off-hours.

That's why I originally experimented with call answering services as the installable *product* that could optimize my clients' intake system.

I will say, they were great at answering the phone quickly and professionally. They improved many of our clients' results based on that alone. However, they didn't give anyone the astronomical growth potential of a fully optimized intake system I was seeing with my highest-performing clients.

The largest issue was that when I implemented call answering services our clients' conversion rates dropped. Call answering services often come off as robotic. They also lack empathy and struggle to make the human connection necessary to sell consultations in many areas of law. If your clients are struggling in the face of a work injury or a divorce, call answering services can be disastrous. I took a work call during my wedding anniversary trip to kill off this experiment, it was going so badly.

I went back to the drawing board. I needed something that would get us the best of both worlds—the consistency of a call answering service with the human connection of a dedicated receptionist.

Here's what I did and what I recommend you do as well:

THE IDEAL SOLUTION

1. **Outsource Picking Up the Phone:** Have every single call answered quickly, 24/7, by an outsourced call answering service. If you approach calls this way, you'll ensure 97 percent of your calls are answered (that's what most of our call answering services achieve). There, you've got your consistency.

2. **Forward New Leads to an Internal Staff Member:** Tell the call answering service to handle all new potential client calls by forwarding them to your receptionist or other internal staff member. The rest of the calls you receive they handle on their own, via a detailed flowchart that tells them what you want said and done.

3. **Dedicate Your Receptionist as an Intake Specialist:** Now that the majority of your day-to-day calls are outsourced, your receptionist can focus purely on being awesome at converting new leads into booked consultations. This heavily reduces the call volume they need to handle and makes it possible for them to specialize in doing whatever it takes to sell the consultation.

That final point is important. The biggest advantage of a dedicated intake specialist is that they can implement the best intake practices possible.

That leads us to step two.

STEP TWO: OPTIMIZE THE CONSULTATION OFFER

The most challenging goal for the EBDS was to make a product that didn't require my customers *or their teams* to learn anything. Telling a law firm's intake team, whether outsourced or internal, to watch a long training course was directly against my product's objective. I needed to create something they could download into their business immediately.

So, I agreed to work for free.

I partnered with my customers' intake teams (both outsourced and internal) to experiment with different ways of selling their consultations, including how much they should charge. Then, I wrote scripts that our customers' call answering services and intake specialists could follow. I automized their new lead follow-up and determined how to make our consultation booking system scalable for explosive growth.

As a result, I discovered that we could consistently get 35 to 50 percent of leads to convert into consultations.

I recommend you aim for the same numbers and that you do it in the same way.

Aim to close at least 35 percent of potential clients into consultations by training your intake specialist to consistently follow your scripts. Call answering services and receptionists find it much easier to follow a successful script than to undergo sales training. And I find it's often much more effective as well. By following a script, you'll also be able to collect data on what works and what doesn't for your leads, which will help you tweak your consultation offer for optimal results.

Lastly, there's one final factor you need to know to optimize your intake, something that is fundamental to making our Perfect Intake System product achieve the conversion rates it does.

STEP THREE: FOLLOW UP ON LEADS

Before I left to start my own company, while I was still director of operations, I began watching the sales guys I'd hired try to improve their sales numbers. COVID had blown our marketing through the roof, but the company didn't have anything in place to handle the massively increased call volume.

The salesmen were scrambling, often not calling a lead back for a *week*, and they discovered something mind-blowing.

If they called back within five minutes after a lead had contacted them, they converted twenty-one times better than if they attempted the same call a half hour later.

Why? Because their potential new client had already called, spoken to, and hired another agency in that time frame.

As far as I can tell, this is even more true for attorneys. My pet theory is that it's because an attorney's clients are typically under extreme stress when they contact a lawyer. It takes them a while to build up the nerve to make the search for an attorney in the first place, and once they've gotten started, they will not sit in that anxiety and wait, even to leave a voicemail.

They will hire an attorney *fast* and, 70 percent of the time, that is the first attorney they speak with.

To combat that, you *must* have aggressive call follow-up systems in place. You have to connect with leads at the moment they're ready to move forward.

Here's what I built into my Perfect Intake System:

- **Automatic form lead follow-up:** Any lead who has filled out an online form but not booked a consultation is automatically called, texted, and emailed until they do (or until they remove themselves from our system).

- **Automatic missed call tracking and callback:** All missed calls immediately (and automatically) trigger an alert to either our call answering services or an office intake specialist to call them back.

- **Automatic no-show follow-up:** Any lead who does not show up to their scheduled consultation is automatically called, texted, and emailed until they reschedule their consultation (or until they remove themselves from our system).

I love this product. I love putting it in place. It is a simple *install*, with no advanced sales training or slow hiring processes necessary. My clients' lives get *easier*, and they make more money.

You can get these same results, and there are many call tracking and automation software out there to work with.

It's so worth it.

One of my clients, Andrew Donovan, nearly doubled his call-to-consultation conversion rate just by putting this into place.

CORE COMPONENT NUMBER THREE: THE SALES BLUEPRINT SYSTEM

I now had my clients generating abundant leads, converting 35 to 50 percent of their leads into booked consultations, and automatically following up with those new leads to ensure they attended the consultations. The first and second core components—marketing and intake, were optimized.

However, do you remember when I said that I listened in on my clients' consultation calls? Both my struggling clients and my explosive success stories?

The difference between them was palpable, and this time, I knew I had my work cut out for me.

I quickly discovered that while law schools may do an excellent job of teaching their students about the law, they do not even attempt to teach them about sales. As insane as it was to me, not a single lawyer I spoke to had ever been required to take a class on closing a prospective law firm client. Nor had they even been *offered* one.

Worse, many legal associations have made attorneys feel like good sales practices are manipulative and cold-hearted. Some of the lawyers I worked with were deeply uncomfortable with the thought of improving their sales approach.

I saw the evidence of that immediately. My struggling lawyers would spend hours of their time giving out free legal advice on a consultation without even *mentioning* their sales offer, and would often hang up without doing so. Most of them didn't think about consultations as a sales call at all. If they did press for a sale, they did it at the very end, dropping a giant retainer number like $20,000 without advocating for it.

They were converting very few of these calls into cases. They would do better with referrals, but nothing even close to what I knew was possible for them.

Now, that presented quite a challenge for me.

I retained my goal for an entirely *installable* business development product that would optimize a business's three core components.

That brought me back to sales scripts, follow-up, and outsourcing. This time, I wasn't optimizing an intake team trying to sell a free or low-cost consultation. Now, I needed to write a script that would work for an attorney attempting to sell a $20,000 retainer.

Again, I worked for free, wrestling with the constraints of the legal field to create a sales product that worked, and worked for *any* field of law.

After two years, I'd gotten it to work, and let me tell you, that product changed peoples' lives.

Let me show you the *first step* of the Sales Blueprint System, what we call the From Hell-to-Heaven Consultation Script.

STEP ONE: THE "FROM HELL TO HEAVEN" CONSULTATION

There are three phases of a successful consultation: (1) help the potential new client understand their pain (Hell), (2) give them a vision of life with all of their goals obtained (Heaven), and (3) offer a clear path out of their pain and to their goals (the Bridge from Hell to Heaven):

HELL

At the start of every consultation, whether you want them to or not, every potential client will start telling you all about their life problems—their personal Hell. This puts a lot of emotional weight on you as a lawyer, but trust me when I say it's a *good thing*.

You need to understand someone's starting point to help them get to where they want to be. It also builds rapport between you and your potential client. You can begin to bond.

This is the part of a good sales-oriented consultation that almost every lawyer I've met has going well, albeit, usually too well.

Most attorneys dread consultations because they offer *far* too much of this part of the consultation, and they don't know how to move it along. As a result, they dread consultations and fear that their potential clients will take them for granted and demand both free advice and free therapy.

That's not good for their mental health, and it's horrendous for their sales results. It's not good for the potential client either.

Remember, clients go to lawyers for help, usually in navigating a complex, high-stakes, stressful engagement like a major financial purchase or a complex, heart-wrenching, stressful negotiation like a lawsuit or a divorce. It does not serve them well to pour their hearts out to someone and then hang up any more than it helps the lawyer who takes that call.

That's where the next step of the script comes in. It is the section that many attorneys come to look forward to within their consultations because the conversation lightens, and they get to see where they could be of genuine assistance to the potential client.

HEAVEN

As you might guess, Heaven is the opposite of Hell. In this part of the consultation, lead your potential client to discuss their ideal vision for what their life would look like twelve months from now.

It's a life where not only their "Hell" issues are resolved, but they've also achieved greater goals that make them happy again.

This is arguably the most important part of the consultation. It's also the area where most lawyers spend the least amount of time because they're afraid of offering a guarantee of results, even accidentally.

Now, that makes sense, but that's why it's essential to script the conversation such that you're gathering information *from* your potential client, not saying anything *to* them. You need to know what a client *wants* to have for any hope of giving it to them. And how could you advise your client on approaching their problem if you don't know what solution to aim for? That's not a guarantee of results; that's the very beginning of mutual strategizing.

Get this right and your potential client will begin to feel like you know what they want. Now, you can turn your focus to the final section of your script to help your client determine whether you're the right fit to help them work toward Heaven.

BRIDGE

The bridge is your service, specifically, where you pitch your services as a bridge to escape the client's current Hell and walk toward Heaven. You do this *before* asking for the sale.

Here's what you need to know: no one buys a lawyer. No one buys your law degree. They buy *help*. They buy a service that they believe will pull them out of the chaos of their "Hell" and point them toward their "Heaven" goals.

In this section of the script, you make 100 percent certain that your client understands how your services could help them out of the Hell they're in and how it would point them toward the Heaven they want.

Then you tell them how much that service costs and ask for the sale. Why? Because at that point, they'll be certain that they want it.

That's not manipulation. That's helping your potential clients understand what your service does and how you can help them.

Step Two takes us further into optimization.

STEP TWO: REPLACE YOURSELF

You must understand that eight-figure law firm owners aren't doing their own consultations. To scale to eight figures, you must stop trading your time for money.

To do that, you'll need to create the scripts and frameworks I've taught you to train either an associate attorney or a non-attorney to take your consultations.

I'm an advocate for having an associate specialize exclusively in selling your services and *not* fulfilling them. While the Sales Blueprint System can make anyone have great sales results even without sales skills, you will get even *better* results if someone on your team can specialize.

In addition, this person can handle even more consultations if they're not distracted with client work. They will *more* than pay for their hourly rate if they're closing deals and ensuring that *you* don't have to be a salesperson for the company.

That leads us to the final step: Automating your follow-up.

STEP THREE: AUTOMATE YOUR FOLLOW-UP

Did you know 50 percent or more of deals won't close after the first conversation? This is where most of the lawyers I worked with gave up. I knew that if I was going to optimize my customers' sales, that needed to change. And it needed to change without them putting in any more effort. Their job was to manage their law firm's explosive growth; my job was to give their business that explosive growth.

Automation is *essential* for this. If you want to grow explosively, you'll need to either learn how to automate your sales follow-up or outsource it.

You can always use automation to follow up by text and email, but if you've outsourced your call answering services while optimizing your intake, you can also do phone follow-up. Don't underestimate the advantages in that; it's far more effective to call someone than to text them.

This means that for our customers, any potential client who has attended a consultation but has yet to sign the engagement letter is automatically called, texted, and emailed until they sign (or until they remove themselves from our system). I highly recommend you set up your own call answering services or have an internal staff member to do similarly.

Follow up heavily during the first two weeks, at a more moderate rate for the two weeks after, and then lightly every month after that. Until you get a definitive *yes* or *no*, or you've disqualified them as a potential client, your job isn't done yet.

THE HIDDEN BENEFIT

The Sales Blueprint System has a hidden benefit: it makes your law firm more sellable.

You stop being the key person holding down the company's consultations and follow-up, which means that someone can estimate what your business is worth even without you in it!

I don't say that idly. For many of my customers, the ability to sell their firm and retire is a massive factor in their sense of personal success and financial freedom. It's the proof that they've made something bigger than themselves, more than a career; they've made an elite, explosively successful *business* that someone else values to the tune of millions of dollars.

If you still don't think that that's available to you, let me introduce you to Everly Kensington.

MEET EVERLY KENSINGTON

When Everly started working with us, she was nearly in bankruptcy. She was trapped and insolvent. She was spending over $1500 a month on SEO marketing, which was frequently giving her fewer than ten leads a month. Her intake was great, but each consultation lasted over an hour and a half, and she would count herself lucky to close 15 percent of them. She had to let staff go. She was nearing retirement age but was far from having the choice to retire.

We optimized her marketing and started receiving fifty leads per month within four months. We gave her our Sales Blueprint System script for consultations, and she began to close 35 percent of her leads in thirty minutes or less. For any lead that didn't close, our automation followed up with them, and she started closing clients from consultations she'd given six months before.

She's now considering selling her law firm, and her business is worth enough that retirement is a choice she could make any day she chooses.

That's the power of optimized sales when it's combined with good marketing and intake. That's the power of the three core components.

YOU'RE ONE SYSTEM AWAY

I told you before that the EBDS can radically change your law firm. That's true. That's truer than I think I could ever convince you to believe until you see your law firm begin to crush its competitors and pull away into another league. However, there's a human side to business that most people never get to see. The success of your business is a major contributor to what life you get to live.

Do you have a chauffeur take you into town, or do you drive yourself? Do you have a personal chef prepare your family meals? Do you retire early? Do you attend business summits with some of the greatest attorneys of our age?

Whatever your dream is, you're one system away from achieving it. The EBDS can get you there. The question is only whether or not you do it.

However, if you don't feel like you *can* implement the EBDS, I know you *won't* implement it.

That's why I want to take the whole next chapter to teach you how you can implement the EBDS, *one step at a time.*

I mean it—one step at a time—and on step three, you'll start making money.

I doubt you'll be surprised to hear I have a system for it.

CHAPTER THREE

THE EFFORTLESS IMPLEMENTATION SYSTEM

When I started consulting, I was downright dumb about helping other people. I thought I could help my attorneys by telling them what I *knew* they needed to change in their law firms. This was boneheaded of me, especially when I *knew* how overwhelmed my clients were just keeping up with the daily thrumming of their businesses.

I'd give them a dozen suggestions on where they could optimize their marketing, intake, and sales and be surprised when my clients were stuck in court, working on their clients' cases, or struggling with their customer relationship management (CRM) updates.

Eventually—and I'm the first to admit it took me too long—I figured out what it meant to *really* help people.

> And that meant entering their world, understanding what they needed, and making something that made their lives *easier*.

I went back to the drawing board and started figuring out in-house, automated, and outsourced services that eventually became The Elite Business Development System. Nowadays, this gives my customers a complete Done-For-Them install, requiring less than an hour of their personal time. And that helped the attorneys who were able to pay for my help. However, as I'll talk about in a bit, I only work with a few attorneys at a time, which left a large group of law firms struggling, feeling too overwhelmed to implement the EBDS even if they did know about it.

That's why I set out to develop the Effortless Implementation System. I wanted to create a step-by-step approach that meant implementing the EBDS was both eminently approachable and would even *assist* an attorney's general business anxiety.

I've heard it said that education is about balancing order and wonder. Adding *wonder* in business was easy for me. I find every bit of it exciting, and it's downright electric to watch hope and big dreams return to my clients' eyes. Adding *order*, however, took cutting down all my grand ideas and seemingly endless to-do lists and learning to triage them.

One thing. I set that as my goal. What would I tell a law firm if I could only direct them to change *one thing?*

That became a series of steps, each one leading to the next. And to my delight, my customers started implementing stress-free changes, jumping from one step to the next with ease. They got the EBDS fully implemented almost without noticing they'd done it. The Effortless Implementation System adds a sense of order and control to your business development and almost *incidentally* makes your law firm better.

Let me run you through the Effortless Implementation System step-by-step.

> Remember, you only need
> to start with **Step One**.

STEP ONE: A CRYSTAL-CLEAR TRACKING SYSTEM

The first goal in implementing The Elite Business Development System is to determine the biggest gaps in your business development system. These are the areas where small tweaks will have the biggest outcome.

Without clear data, it's impossible to know where the gaps are and how to address them. You'll start like I always do with my new customers: data tracking.

Your tracking system should track all your leads, calls, and consultations.

You're looking to determine three vital statistics:

1. How many leads you are generating each month

2. How many of your leads are turning into consultations

3. How many of those consultations are turning into cases

These three vital statistics give you a crystal-clear image of how well your marketing, intake, and sales systems are doing.

STEP TWO: FIND A QUICK, BIG WIN

Now compare your data to the results you'd expect with a fully implemented Elite Business Development System. Those are:

1. Total Lead Count (see note below):

    a. Eighty-five calls/month for a $1 Million Dollar Law Firm (annual revenue).

    b. Four hundred twenty-five calls per month for a $5 Million Dollar Law Firm (annual revenue).

    c. Eight hundred fifty calls per month for a $10 Million Dollar Law Firm (annual revenue).

2. Thirty-five percent or more of leads convert to consultations.

3. Thirty-five percent or more of consultations are converted into cases.

Note: This is assuming an average case value (ACV) of $8,000. If your ACV is lower than that, expect to need more leads, and vice versa. That said, if your ACV is lower than $3000, I usually recommend raising your prices outside of certain exceptions such as real estate law.

When you're clear on the data and know where the biggest gaps are, you can focus on the one change that will address the largest issue first.

Keep in mind, I said *one*. The *one* change that will address the largest issue first.

Don't make the mistake of trying to fix everything right away. I know it's tempting because you want the explosive results fully implementing the EBDS will get you.

However, you would get the best results now by focusing on the most obvious way to improve your profit. First of all, when you focus on the biggest issues, you get the quickest wins. Once you've gotten your first quick win, it'll become much easier to implement everything else in the EBDS. You'll know with the confidence of conclusive proof that it's worth your time and resources.

Secondarily, you'll get time working for you. We've all heard the example of the best time to plant a tree—twenty years ago. And the second-best time is today. You want to start implementing changes in a way that gets you the most money the quickest.

Once you have more revenue, you'll have more money to work with to implement the next biggest win, and you'll have far more motivation to do so. Trust me, it'll snowball from there until you have the whole system implemented. I'll discuss that more in step four.

That being said, don't try to do everything yourself! That's where the next step comes in.

STEP THREE: OUTSOURCE OR HIRE WHENEVER POSSIBLE

Once you know what you need to implement, I recommend you *own the strategy*. Outsource or hire out the grunt work wherever possible.

What do I mean by *own the strategy*? I mean, you would take responsibility for the results by customizing your scripts and templates, but you don't do all the actual work, like answering your own phones.

The same is true for marketing. Own the strategy for your marketing, but you don't need to do everything yourself. You can hire someone else to execute it. That goes for sales as well.

Obviously, you need to own the strategy, but you can hire someone to do it.

The EBDS generally works best when you focus on your areas of strength and let others do the tasks that don't require you to do them personally. It was, after all, designed from the ground up so that my business could do it for our customers as a 100 percent remote, installable product. You *can* do it all yourself. That said, I truly don't recommend it.

Hire enough out, and you'll find the EBDS almost implements itself.

There's a second big factor here, other than just ease: time. Usually, a specialist will be faster to implement a change than you ever will be. Do you need your GBP optimized and maintained? It would require many hours a week for you to do yet is only a short phone call away to outsource.

Don't forget: If you're not growing exponentially right now, you're likely leaving tens of thousands of dollars on the table due to the gaps in your business development system.

That means that every day you spend *not fixing it* likely costs far more than the price of fixing it. That's what it means to improve systems that make you money—*not* doing so *costs* you money.

Find the fastest route to get that first win, and you'll get that snowball rolling.

STEP FOUR: RINSE AND REPEAT

Once you've discovered your gaps through the Effortless Implementation System, chosen a gap to focus on, and hired out what you could to fix it, you're likely to get a quick win, such as a huge uptick in scheduled consultations or signed cases.

After that first win, celebrate! You have proof that I know what I'm talking about, and that explosive growth can be understood, and your law firm can grow to crush all of its competitors and join the elite few standing at the top of their field.

Now, it's time to take that energy and recommit. Start again at Step One of the Effortless Implementation System. Take a look at your latest data, pick the next biggest issue to solve, hire it out where you can, and roll toward another big win.

You'll then use that energy to get the next quick win, the next one, the next one, and so on.

Then, just keep doing those quick wins until you've implemented the full Elite Business Development System.

Here's an example of what that could look like for you:

Let's say you're getting 300 leads per month but struggling to make a profit. Your biggest issue would not be marketing; you've got plenty of leads. Your biggest issue is either intake or sales, so you look at how your phones are answered, how your leads convert to consultations, and how your consultations are conducted. Let's say you have a 30 percent call-to-consultation rate but a 5 percent conversion rate in your consultations to paid cases. That sales rate is further off from the EBDS standards than your marketing or intake numbers. So, you choose sales as the area to focus on. You hire someone like me to provide a sales script for you and begin to follow it during your calls.

Let's say that brings up your sales rate to a 25 percent conversion from consultations to cases. Now you have money coming in five times faster than you did before. You pop open a bottle of champagne, buy something you could never have afforded before, and take a fresh look at your data, to see if more leads, better intake, or a stronger sales rate reveal the biggest gap, and the next quickest win.

MEET JANET SLOANE

Let me introduce you to one of my former clients, Janet Sloane. She is a perfect example of how the Effortless Implementation System can give you results despite a highly frantic schedule and an anxious mind.

When I met her, Janet had very few leads, missed almost all her calls, and was barely booking any consultations. She was leading a small firm and couldn't make changes very fast. The idea of implementing the EBDS was far too overwhelming to contemplate.

That's where the Effortless Implementation System really shone. She was only ever dealing with one change to her law firm at a time.

The first change was to her tracking so we could look for her biggest gap. It was far and away that she didn't have enough lead flow. We implemented the Marketing Mastery System and tripled her lead volume in a couple of months. As a note, we did add GBP and Google Ads at the same time, but because this was outsourced to us, *she* only needed to take one action. Hire our firm.

The next big gap was in her intake system. We focused on this instead of sales because she was doing decently well with sales. The trouble was that she never had the chance to *make* a sale because she wasn't meeting with any potential clients.

We outsourced and automated everything: Her phone calls, her follow-up, her consultation scheduling, everything. Her direct line rarely rang. All she saw were consultations popping up on her calendar. As a result, she quadrupled her intake rate of turning calls into consultations, bringing it from about 10 to 40 percent.

At that point, Janet was getting enough consultations that it was worth it to start improving her sales system. She began selling only paid consultations and is now maintaining a 30 percent conversion rate.

Over about nine months, we systematically implemented every single component of The Elite Business Development System.

The key, though, is that we did it one piece at a time, with very little stress. One change at a time—one *win* at a time.

I love this simple, low-stress implementation style because I get to watch as my clients' lives change right before their eyes. Their businesses start to grow as soon as they implement the first change. Even more than the money, though, I think it's the easy and steady progress that brings the hope and fun back into business for them.

The success that felt impossible for so long is suddenly unfolding for them, and it's under their control—one understandable *and purchasable* step at a time.

Quick wins, excitement, control, and better cash flow. What's not to love?

There's only one thing that gives my potential customers pause, and in the case that it's worrying you, too, it's what I address in the next chapter.

What if I'm not ready for that level of growth right now?

CHAPTER FOUR

THE GROWTH CONTROL SYSTEM

It took me a while to learn that not everyone *wanted* astronomical growth, or at least not all the time. As a kid, I desperately wanted breakout success in business, and, like a kid, I didn't understand that there's an ebb and flow to growth and consolidation.

After I launched The Elite Business Development System, I experienced something I never had before.

Clients were canceling with me because I'd been *too successful*.

Their calendar was booked by too many consultations for them to handle, especially given how many new cases they'd already signed on, and they couldn't hire fast enough to fill in the gaps, especially when they were struggling to find the time to arrange interviews with associate attorney applicants.

I had a problem on my hands. How could I help my clients who needed the time to breathe and consolidate before committing to more growth?

I needed ways to dial marketing, intake, and sales up or down for more or less output, and over time, I learned which dials were easy to turn off, and back on again, and which were better left alone.

Now, you can set your desired growth rate.

You never need to feel like the EBDS is galloping away with you.

Everything I've taught you so far pertains to cranking up the EBDS *up* for maximum growth.

Here are the three steps to increasingly dial the EBDS back *down*.

They're in the order I recommend you follow. I'll explain my reasoning as I walk through them step-by-step.

To get us started, if you want to grow slower, the first thing I'd recommend is to throttle your intake process.

STEP ONE: DIAL DOWN INTAKE

There are two good methods to throttle your intake, and both will improve your quality of life. The *first* is to increase the strictness of your lead quality. This means instructing your intake specialist to ask more questions of the leads calling in and give them standards to inform the lead when you're unable to take their case, all without you ever stepping into a consultation. I recommend demographic details, such as household income, or case details, such as the number of assets involved, to attempt to filter lower-paying leads out of your system early.

The *second* method is to increase your consultation price. This also often sorts for higher-quality leads, as motivated and wealthy potential clients won't price balk as quickly as less motivated, lower-income leads.

I recommend starting by increasing the strictness of your lead quality because you're throttling based on proven factors rather than risking losing good leads who simply aren't ready to put down money yet. That said, if you've already increased your lead quality strictness as much as you wish to, then upping your consultation price is always an available option.

After that, however, if you still want to slow down your growth curve, I'd recommend you look outside of intake. That brings us to step two, Dial Down Sales.

STEP TWO: DIAL DOWN SALES

When it comes to dialing back your sales, there's one best method. It's so much better than the other options, in fact, that I don't recommend any others. That's this: Up your pricing.

I find many attorneys find this idea quite intimidating. The American Bar Association's (ABA) guideline on *reasonable pricing* is vague and initially alarming. However, I've learned that if a law firm has the lead flow to support it, the greatest thing an attorney can do for their sense of joy in their work is to up their pricing. The benefits are myriad: less work for more money, more respectful clients, and a higher sense of self-worth.

Look at the salaries of the highest-status attorneys in the world: the divorce attorneys who work for celebrities, or the tort attorneys who are called in for the highest-profile lawsuits. At some point, they decided they were worth millions of dollars per case. You can decide for yourself what your work is worth, and if you have dozens of leads knocking at your door wanting your services, it's a good sign that your work is worth a lot.

You can feel confident to up your pricing whenever you're ready.

STEP THREE: DIAL DOWN MARKETING

You probably think it's odd to leave cutting down marketing until last. Most people think that's the first thing to cut when you want to dial down your growth. But here's why I highly recommend you filter for higher quality cases and set higher prices first:

I believe one of the most important factors in the success of an attorney is their state of mind. I've seen it time and time again. I take on a client who is feeling run down, undervalued, overworked, and hopeless about their business's growth, and watch what happens when I put the Marketing Mastery System in place for them. Once they have people requesting their services often, they begin to lift their heads up, taking joy in their work and looking for more opportunities to grow. They begin to make better decisions, hire better, and put off retirement because they *want* to run their law firms longer.

Everyone loves cherry-picking their clients. You can only do that when more potential clients are asking for your services than you can serve.

> Good marketing can determine whether or not a business is fun, and I think it's important to maintain a mental state of abundance.

So, I recommend you avoid throttling your marketing until you've throttled everything else, and even then, I say reduce it, *never* cut it. I've always regretted cutting all my marketing. It always leads to a lull, and lulls are depressing.

However, if you've increased your lead strictness as much as you can, upped your consultation prices, upped your own pricing, and *still* want to dial down your marketing …

Here's how:

Start with your Google Ad Budget. The nice thing about Google Ads is that you can reduce the Ad Budget one day and bring it back up the next. That's a flexibility GPB and Webinars don't have.

Next, I'd reduce your webinar ad budget. I put this after Google Ads because webinars have a huge effect on your GBP optimization, due to how many reviews webinars send to your GBP profile.

As you can probably tell from the fact that I left it to the absolute last, I don't recommend throttling your GBP campaign unless you absolutely have to. GBP gives the most bang for your buck, with the least financial investment, and it's the most damaged by inconsistency. GBP can have a ridiculously effective return on investment (ROI) once it's at its peak. However, it only has that effect after it's had a while to get going.

I do want to reiterate that I don't recommend that you cut either your Google Ads, GBP, or Webinars entirely. The fact is these marketing methods rely on consistency and have compounding results over time. By cutting them entirely, you lose most, if not all, of the momentum you've built up, and restarting is challenging and slow. It is better to throttle intake and sales to a strangulation point than kill off your marketing.

YOU HAVE CONTROL

Keep in mind, this is not a single set-and-done decision. The Elite Business Development System for Law Firms can accelerate your business into that $10,000,000+, eight-figure status, in a matter of years. It can also give you a steady, gentle growth curve. Or, as most of my clients choose, it can be throttled up and down for alternating periods of growth and consolidation on the way to greatness. Either way, it can keep you crushing your competitors and peers.

CHAPTER FIVE

ARE YOU READY?

Congratulations! You've now learned almost everything I can teach you in a book about The Elite Business Development System for Law Firms and how to implement it to reach your dreams.

I'm not exaggerating when I say this system can change the destiny of your law firm—and, if you wish it to, the course of your life!

Now let me ask you a question:

- If you marketed your law firm with the three assets that drive 87 percent of leads, as I showed you with the Marketing Mastery System … *and*

- you automated your intake process with the Perfect Intake System … *and*

- you doubled your sales closing rate by implementing the Sales Blueprint System …

… do you think you'd be on track to break eight figures with your law firm?

And now, a second question:

Do you want to do it yourself?

In this book, I've included everything needed to make sure you get results. I want you to succeed far more than I want you to succeed *with me.* That said, the contents of this book do not make an installable product like The Elite Business Development System for Law Firms was designed to be. It will take work on your part— work that I'm certain will pay for itself in ninety days if you implement the EBDS correctly—but work all the same.

If doing that work yourself sounds good to you, it's totally fine if you close the book here. I've taught you everything I can in this format, and I think you're well-positioned to crush your competitors with your law firm. I wish you the very best! Before you go, if you think this book has helped your business, please leave a review to help me reach other attorneys so they can also learn how to build world-caliber businesses!

However, if you want to outsource implementing the EBDS, *and* you want the fastest growth curve possible, I've created a special package offer to have my team expertly install it in your business ASAP.

I don't work with all clients that come to me, but I give a high priority to those who have read this book, so if you would like to work with me, keep reading.

QUICK FAVOR

I'm wondering, did you enjoy this book?

Thank you for reading *The Elite Business Development System for Law Firms*. May I ask a quick favor?

Would you kindly take a moment and leave your honest review? Reviews are the single best way to help others discover—and benefit from—this book.

**Please leave your review
at NoBullMarketing.com/Review**

CHAPTER SIX

OUR OFFER AND PROMISE

A TESTED & PROVEN SYSTEM

I've spent years working with my clients, perfecting the methods I discussed in this book and learning how to optimize them for each area of law, from real estate to estate planning. I tested different implementation styles and vendors, created the intake and sales templates and scripts, and all of the Done-For-You services involved.

I'm thrilled to offer you the end product that I've tested and proven on hundreds of clients. What you're getting now is the culmination of all that trial and error.

You don't have to wait to figure things out. There's no learning curve required, period. You will get the benefits of a fully optimized Elite Business Development System right away, tailored to the growth curve you'd like to see.

Most importantly:

The average lawyer spends less than sixty minutes with our team implementing the entire system. Everything else is done for you.

Even better, it starts right away.

In the thirty days after you've signed onto The Elite Business Development System for Law Firms package, you'll be able to:

- Reliably trace 100 percent of your leads from their initial source all the way to the day they sign with you.

- Generate more leads effectively on autopilot (no dancing on TikTok required!).

- Relax in confidence as your leads are consistently nurtured and converted into consultations.

- Improve your sales process and enjoy a greater consultation-to-case conversion rate, meaning more money coming into your firm without delay.

Within ninety days, you could be:

- Living without anxiety, certain where your next case will come from.

- Easily closing 30 percent, 50 percent, or even 80 percent of your consultations into paying clients.

- Making more money than ever.

- On track to reach eight figures in a matter of years while maintaining a joyous lifestyle.

Here's what I'll include to get that done:

1. **Our Done-For-You Marketing Mastery System: The essential trio of assets to triple your lead volume.**

   - **Lead Tracking Complete.** Every lead, be it from a call, form, live chat, or email, we track. We identify their source, discover their journey, and trace every new consultation and case back to its origin. This empowers you to make smarter decisions about what's working and what's not.

   - **Google Business Profile Domination.** Unlock GMB's full potential with us. We don't just optimize; we dominate. We outclass competitors with our proactive management, posts, photos, Q&As, review responses, and more. It's not set-it-and-forget-it. It's set-it, manage-it, and crush-it for maximum results.

- **ProfitMint Precision Google Ads.** With relentless dedication, industry-specific insights, and high-conversion landing pages, it's not just about running ads. It's about minting profit. Turn Google Ads into your personal money-printing machine with laser-focused precision.

- **Evergreen Webinar Pro.** Maximize profits, skyrocket reviews, and dominate your niche with evergreen Done-For-You webinars.

This is a $240,000 Per Year Total Value

2. **Our Done-For-You Perfect Intake System:** Effortlessly manage limitless leads and consistently convert over 35 percent into consultations, thanks to better documentation, scripts, outsourcing, and automation.

- **Intake Mapping.** Shield your intake process from inconsistency with an unshakable digital asset, mapping out foolproof call handling for every situation, ensuring unwavering reliability and success.

- **Sales Mastery via Intake.** Transform your intake calls into sales powerhouses. Present your consultation as a valuable offer, not a roadblock, and witness a skyrocketing booking rate with ease.

- **Outsourced Call Answering Setup & Ongoing Training.** Seamlessly merging with your internal systems, our outsourced call answering partners register a mere 3 percent missed call rate against the usual 22 percent and regularly convert upwards to 35 percent of leads into booked consultations. No unanswered or mishandled calls, just more consultation bookings.

- **Automated Booked Calendar System.** With swift automated action through text, call, and email follow-up, our Automated Booked Calendar System encourages leads to book a consultation immediately and attend so no-shows become a worry of the past!

This is a $32,000 Per Year Total Value

3. **Our Done-For-You Sales Blueprint System:** Close Up To 80 percent of Consultations with one Simple Framework, Sales Scripts, and Intelligent Automation; No Sales Skills Required.

- **The "From Hell-to-Heaven" Consultation Framework.** Master our three-step sales framework to maximize efficiency, control consultations, and clinch deals faster. Say goodbye to unproductive free advice sessions and gain command over post-consultation closes. No prior sales expertise is needed.

- **The "From Hell-to-Heaven" Sales Scripts.** Unlock our arsenal of high-impact, practice-specific consultation scripts that incorporate the Hell-to-Heaven Consultation Framework. Implement instantly and witness your consultation conversions skyrocket.

Sign an unprecedented numbers of engagement letters today!

- **Sign Fast Automations.** Deploy assertive but courteous automated follow-ups after consultations. Utilize texts, calls, and emails to motivate and remind each consultee to promptly sign the engagement letter.

- **Hand-in-Hand Continuous Training & Support.**
  - **Unlimited Sales Call Audits** - Submit recordings of your sales calls to receive pinpoint feedback and strategic action plans to guarantee your sales momentum continues to thrive.
  - **Lifetime Sales Script Updates** - Get access to every new sales script we develop, now and in the future, for all practice areas.

This is a $50,000 Per Year Total Value

Remember: The average lawyer spends less than sixty minutes with our team implementing the entire system. Everything else is done for you.

EBDS = $322,000 Per Year Total Value

WOULD IT BE WORTH IT?

I'm not going to charge you $322,000 per year to do all this.

But if I did charge $322,000 per year, and all this system did was generate $1,000,000 per year in new revenue, would it be worth it to you?

That question answers itself and builds out from there.

⇨ If *all* this system did was generate 300 leads per month or 3,600 leads per year, would it be worth it?

⇨ If *all* this system did was double your number of scheduled consultations, would it be worth it?

⇨ If *all* this system did was triple your sales close rate from 20 percent to 60 percent or more, would it be worth it?

⇨ If *all* this system did was make it possible to reach eight figures in a matter of years in a systematic, stress-free way, asking nothing but an hour of your time, would it be worth it?

The answer is yes! But it doesn't just do one—the EBDS does *all* of this!

By now, you've seen the results of many of my clients who have done over $1,000,000 in new revenue in their first year and have achieved that eight-figure status, without spending more than an hour of their own time.

You can see why those law firms have paid me hundreds of thousands of dollars for these services.

Why? Because it's not a cost, it's an *investment*.

ONLY TWO AT A TIME

After I'd finished creating the EBDS, and after I'd tested it with a variety of law firms, including *Guardian & Baron*, who had lackluster lead volume, Andrew Donovan, who had unreliable intake, and Everly Kensington, whose sales system was in shambles, I knew it was ready to launch.

I then had a choice in my hands:

How many firms did I think I could help at a time?

At first, it appealed to me to try to help as many law firms as possible. It *hurts* to watch a law firm flounder when I know perfectly well how to make that attorney's dreams come true.

However, the problem with that approach was that I couldn't devote myself fully to driving the incredible eight-figure results I knew were possible for the law firms that work with me.

So, I decided to limit myself and make this system exclusively available to just two new law firms per month.

JUST TWO

I can't help as many lawyers, but my team can dedicate themselves to getting to know you and your goals and focus on the initial setup and onboarding required to optimize the EBDS in its first thirty days.

YOUR READER BONUS

I mentioned that I don't work with all the potential clients that wish to work with me. That's very true. However, I know something more about you now:

You've read this far in the book. I most enjoy working with clients who want to grow their businesses and are actively looking for the best ways to do it. So, given that you've gotten this far in a book titled *The Elite Business Development System for Law Firms*, I think I want to work with you.

So even though I can make you millions of dollars and could charge $322,000 or more per year in return, I am going to make you a special offer because you took the time to read this book. Mention in your demo that you've read this book or follow the link I'm about to give you (because, of course, I've added tracking to that), and I'll offer you the pricing listed below. And there's a bonus! If you sign up for The Elite Business Development System Package, my team will work with you to create a One-Year Game Plan to reach your exact financial goals, absolutely free!

That means that you'll get:

- DFY Marketing Mastery System
(Valued at $240,000 per year)

- DFY Perfect Intake System
(Valued at $32,000 Per Year)

- DFY Sales Blueprint System
(Valued at $50,000 Per Year)

- BONUS: The One-Year Game Plan
(Valued at $1,500 Per Year)

That's a total value of $323,500 per year!

You'll get it all for just $12,500 per month - over half off!

All you need to do to get started is go to https://nobullmarketing.com/talk to book your demo with my team.

AN EXTRA $10,000

Remember how I mentioned at the start of this book that if you read to the end, you could save $10,000? When you connect with my team and mention that you've read this book, I will give you another $10,000 off your first year of investment.

Let me put this all into perspective.

It takes more than one marketing professional to implement and maintain The Elite Business Development System in as optimized a way as possible.

Imagine that you were going to hire two average skilled marketing professionals for $80,000 per year. You would spend *more* money than I'm asking you to invest in us. What's worse, those two average marketing people would likely spend the majority of their time doing busy work that leads to *zero* financial growth for your firm in twelve months.

Why? Because those marketers would have *little idea* what they're doing. They haven't put in the blood, sweat, and tears that we have. They haven't spent the time looking at data across law firms to discover what *exactly* optimizes each asset within The Elite Business Development System for Law Firms. Which means they would be losing you money every month.

> By contrast, when you hire my team to install the EBDS,
> you're getting the results
> of nearly a decade of trial and error
> from me and my team.

We have devoted ourselves to the success of over 300 law firms. As a result, we have discovered exactly what works and what doesn't. Our average client ROI in the first ninety days is about three and a half times. In the first twelve months, that number increases to seven times. Beyond that, it's not uncommon for our clients to make over a twelve times ROI on our efforts. For every dollar you spend on us, you could get $12 back. Crazy, right?

TWO CHOICES BEFORE YOU

At this point, you have two choices.

The first is that you can choose to do nothing. If you do nothing with the information you've learned in this book, what will you get?

Nothing.

Or you can choose to take a leap of faith.

Give me three months, and the EBDS will pay back what you've invested in it. Give it a year, and it'll change your life.

Here are the kind of life changes you can expect, within a year.

- **Your INCOME:** You will move from inconsistent results to predictable and scalable revenue.

- **Your SECURITY:** You will move from stress because you're working *in* the business with peace of mind because you're working *on* the business.

- **Your AVERAGE DAY:** You will move from fighting long hours to enjoying a controlled schedule each day.

- **Your STATUS:** You will move from uncertainty to confidence as you go from a struggling law firm to the biggest success of your peer group.

Just test it out to see if it will work for you.

I'm so confident in the quality of our work that I not only guarantee our success, I quadruple guarantee it!

Guaranteed Satisfaction: Not thrilled within the first thirty days? Cancel your contract and get a complete refund, no questions asked.

One-Year Hit-or-Miss Guarantee Stack:

- **Marketing Mastery System Guarantee:** Guaranteed lead volume based on your One-Year Game Plan in twelve months, or you get our services free until we deliver!

- **Perfect Intake System:** Guaranteed 95 percent call pickup rate and a minimum 20 percent lead to consultation conversion rate, or our services are free until we deliver!

- **Sales Blueprint System:** Guaranteed minimum 30 percent consultation-to-case close rate within twelve months, or you pay nothing until you do!"

The options are success or success!

The real question is this: Is it worth gambling a few minutes of your time to check this out? Even if it does only *half* of what I've claimed, it will pay for itself in as little as ninety days.

The next step is to schedule a demo call with my team today. Simply go to nobullmarketing.com/talk or scan the QR code below to book a time and remember to mention this book! My team will provide you with a One-Year Game Plan (valued at $1500) to reach your financial goals, give you an instant $10,000 first-year discount, *and* provide you with the book's exclusive $12,500 per month pricing.

But remember, we *only* take two new law firms per month. If you're at all interested in having my team install The Elite Business Development System into your law firm, I highly encourage you to book your demo call today.

CHAPTER SEVEN

QUESTIONS
AND ANSWERS

After reading about The Elite Business Development System for Law Firms and hearing my offer, you know everything you need to know to maximize the growth of your law firm! However, in this final chapter, I'll dive into some of the most common questions I hear, along with my brief responses.

Does this program really work for all types of business-to-consumer (B2C) law firms? Family law and criminal law are so different. How could one program work for both?

We've worked on over 300 legal marketing campaigns. The likelihood is extremely high that we've worked with multiple law firms in your practice area. We've worked on almost every type of law firm campaign under the sun. The overall structure of the EBDS is flexible enough that we can easily adjust it with our team's deep, specialized knowledge of each practice area to maximize the profitability of any client's campaign.

For example, with Google Ads, if your firm works in Personal Injury, we will want to devote most of our effort to trying to reach low-income demographics. On the flip side, if you're an estate planning attorney, we'll focus on reaching high-income demographics. Defining those demographic thresholds numerically changes based on what city you live in.

Our team is armed with in-depth knowledge of each practice area's ideal client, average case value, seasonality, and sale cycle. Therefore, we can provide exceptional results for any B2C law firm practice area, including Family Law, Criminal Law, Personal Injury, Immigration, Disability, Estate Planning, IP, Employment, Real Estate, and any other type of practice area that serves a consumer (rather than a business).

How does this service integrate into my existing vendors, systems, and processes?

It's as smooth as butter. Our team is very comfortable working alongside other vendors, and we have worked with almost every legal marketing software on the market. We can comfortably execute and fulfill all our promises no matter what other vendors or software you work with.

This sounds great, but what about my specific needs? Is your program one-size-fits-all, or can you meet my firm's unique needs?

Our team will work with you during your demo to create a One-Year Game Plan. This allows us to understand your firm's specific needs and implement our program in a manner that best suits your goals.

This sounds like a lot of work and will require a ton of time and input from me.

The great news is, this is untrue! I worked hard to design this program so that it requires as little as an hour of the firm owner's time for a complete setup.

Of course, I encourage our customers to get more involved to help fine tune the campaign to their unique preferences, but I promise it's not necessary to drive the results.

If I invest in all this stuff right now, will it still be working a year from now? Or will I have to start over?

It will certainly work a year from now! This program was designed to focus on the most evergreen, long-lasting, and principle-guided systems possible.

Is my firm too small for this program? Or maybe too large?

If your firm generates at least $500,000 per year, this program will massively increase your revenue in the next twelve months. That said, we don't take clients who make over $12,000,000 in revenue per year, as this system was not optimized for their growth phase.

What happens if this program doesn't deliver the promised results?

That's exactly what our quadruple guarantees are for! We will make this happen for you, one way or another. If it doesn't deliver on the promised results when we say it will, we don't get paid until it does.

Does this lock me into some absurdly long contract that's impossible to get out of?

Nope! We have an automatically renewing three-month contract. Each quarter, we encourage you to evaluate whether you believe we're making you crazy good money or on the path to doing so. If not, fire us!

This sounds like a great deal, but what's the final cost? What are the hidden fees?

Fortunately, there are no extra fees. The price I listed is the price you pay for *everything* involved in The Elite Business Development System.

The only time that price may change is if you decide you want to spend more on ads because you want to spend more to make more.

If I don't want to implement the complete Elite Business Development System, can I pay you to do just one or two of the systems instead?

Yes! But there's one caveat: our team will need to review your current system to determine whether we can drive the results I promise without the systems you're not interested in.

I don't want to grow too fast and be forced to make bad hires. Can I still control my growth even while working with you?

I feel you one hundred percent. Rest assured, you're *always* in control of your growth. If you feel you're growing too fast, we can slow things down while still making you more money.

THE FUTURE IS BRIGHT

You may have struggled in the past, but you don't have to struggle anymore.

You have the intelligence. You have the work ethic. You have the degree. You have the will and desire. The one thing you were missing was a system to take your law firm to the next level of income and success.

The Elite Business Development System for Law Firms is what you've been missing.

Only Two of You
Can Join Us This Month

Schedule a demo call today:

https://nobullmarketing.com/talk

GRATITUDE

I'm grateful to my wife. Gwen, I know I've already dedicated this book to you, but I'm grateful to you twice. You see straight into my heart, and it seems like magic.

I'm grateful for Kent Sanders, who put in incredible effort to write this book with me. Kent, you read a full-length business book just to help me structure my thoughts the way I wanted. You're phenomenal.

I'm grateful for Honorée Corder, who made publishing a book so approachable. I never thought I could get this done before I met you.

I'm grateful to Jan Roos, who inspired me to write my own book by leading the way with his own. You've helped me along my journey more than you know.

I'm grateful to my team member Jake Davis, whose ability to hold down the fort is the only reason I could take enough time and focus away from running my business to write this book at all. I rely on you every day.

I'm grateful to my team member Oliver Goessler, who teaches me new Google Ads tricks every week. Your cleverness and dedication are awe-inspiring.

I'm grateful to my team member Ashley Diggins, who assisted me with this book every step of the way. You were my primary brainstorming buddy because, as you know better than anyone, I can't think unless I'm talking.

I'm grateful to my team member Cat McManus, who has mastered Google Business Profile and made herself indispensable to Jake and the team. Your ability to see a need and grow to fill it is extraordinary.

WHO IS
RONNIE DEAVER?

You may have heard Ronnie Deaver speaking at the American Bar Association, the National Association of Divorce Professionals, or the Law Firm Growth Summit. A lifelong lover of business, he got his start at the age of twelve, selling lawn mowing services online. After twelve years of mastering business development for everything from electronics recycling to MIT's entrepreneurship program, he entered the world of legal marketing and fell in love with the people in the field. He founded NoBull Marketing and committed to working exclusively with law firms and their owners. He sees business as a lesson in virtue, a mirror given by God to teach a man both who he is and who he can become. The reward for doing so is the money to support his wife and children and give them the biggest lives possible.

Originally from Texas, he now lives in Pennsylvania with his family.

Website: https://nobullmarketing.com/
LinkedIn:
https://www.linkedin.com/in/ronniedeaver/